Slime Safety

- The activities in this book require adult supervision at all times.
- Ingredients may cause skin irritation – we recommend that gloves are worn when making or handling slime and that slime is not handled for prolonged periods of time.
- Always wash your hands and tools with soap and water and disinfect surfaces once you have finished an activity.
- Never eat or taste slime or ingredients unless the activity states that it is safe to do so.
- Make sure that slime is kept away from very young children and pets.
- Slime may stain – wear old clothes and cover surfaces to prevent damage.
- If any slime or slime ingredients come into contact with your eyes, flush well with water.
- Dispose of slime in a waste container in the dustbin – do not put slime down sinks or drains.
- Slime only has a short shelf-life, throw away at the first sign of any mould.
- The publisher shall not be liable or responsible in any respect for any use or application of any information or material contained in this book or any adverse effect, consequence, injury, loss, or damage of any type resulting or arising from, directly or indirectly, the use or application of any information or material contained in this book.

Scholastic Children's Books,
Euston House, 24 Eversholt Street,
London NW1 1DB, UK

A division of Scholastic Ltd
London ~ New York ~ Toronto ~ Sydney ~ Auckland
Mexico City ~ New Delhi ~ Hong Kong

Published in the UK by Scholastic Ltd, 2018
Produced by Cloud King Creative

Trade edition ISBN 978 14071 8924 6
Schools edition ISBN 978 14071 9231 4

Printed in the UK by Bell and Bain Ltd, Glasgow

2 4 6 8 10 9 7 5 3 1

Papers used by Scholastic Children's Books are made from
wood grown in sustainable forests.

www.scholastic.co.uk

Magical

Rainbow

SLIME

SCHOLASTIC

Contents

Simple Slimes

Incredible Slimes

Seasonal Slimes

Crafty Slimes

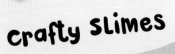

Edible Slimes

We Love Slime!

Fluffy, squeezy, stretchy, colourful, satisfying SLIME! We love the way it feels, looks, smells, sounds, and for certain slimes – even tastes!

In this book you'll find simple recipes to make all sorts of different slimes using simple household ingredients as well as supplies that are easily available online.

We'll explore the science behind slime and find a goo to suit you.

Warning!

Making slime is possibly the coolest science lesson ever! Slime can ooze through your fingers like a liquid, or bounce on a surface like a solid. Remember that the recipes in this book are really chemistry experiments and adults should always supervise any session when you make or play with slime.

Read and remember these simple steps to stay safe and happy when making slime:

* Unless a recipe specifically says that a slime is edible, **do not eat** any slime. The only edible slimes in this book are on pages 84–89: Gummy Bear Slime, Chocolate Slime and Spaghetti Slime.

* Wash your hands well with soap before and after making slime.

* Always keep slime away from pets and very young children.

* Choose paints, glues and other ingredients that are non-toxic and washable.

* Clean any work surfaces before and after making slime.

* If your skin is sensitive, wear protective gloves whenever you touch slime or slime ingredients.

* Keep slime away from all carpets, sofas and other soft materials – wearing old clothes would be wise!

* Throw away any used slime in a waste container in the dustbin – never put slime down sinks or drains.

Slimy science!

The PVA glue used to make slime is a **polymer** – a mixture that is made up of large chains of molecules. When you mix the glue with a slime activator (contact lens solution or laundry detergent containing borate or bicarbonate of soda), slime is formed. The polymers in the activator link with those in the glue and the consistency of the mixture thickens to a goo.

What are you waiting for?

Ready, steady, goo!

Your Slime Shopping List

Making slime is easy, once you know how! If you read ingredients labels and follow the recipes carefully, you should be able to make fantastic slimes in minutes. The slimes in this book can be made using the following ingredients, found in supermarkets, craft shops or online. Always shop online with an adult who can do the ordering for you.

The Base

Clear or white PVA glue: this is sometimes called 'school glue', and clear glue requires less activator than white glue. Whichever glue you use should list PVA (polyvinyl acetate) among its ingredients, be non-toxic and washable.

Activators

Contact lens solution: contact lens solutions or eye drops that contain sodium borate and boric acid should form fantastic slime – check the labels to avoid disappointment. Saline solution is sometimes used to make slime, too.

Bicarbonate of soda: this baking ingredient is added in small amounts to thicken the slime. It can be used with or without contact lens solution as an activator.

Shaving foam: use foam rather than gels to create fluffy slime or flubber (floam).

Liquid laundry detergent: choose a biological detergent that lists boric acid in its ingredients.

Extras

Colours

* **Paints**: use acrylic paints to brighten up your slimes. Colour-changing iridescent shades are dazzling!
* **Food colouring (liquid or gel)**: gels often produce brighter, deeper colours than liquid food colouring and are less messy.
* **Highlighter pens**: for making awesome neon goos.

Extras

* **Glitter**: normal or iridescent glitters give your slime an instant upgrade. Add one or multiple colours.
* **Sequins**: sequins of all shapes, sizes and colours add shimmer and crunch!
* **Beads**: adding glass or plastic beads turns ordinary slime into noisy, crackling slime.
* **Drinking straws**: chop into 1-cm pieces to add crunch to your slime.

Finishes

* **Baby oil or coconut oil**: a drop of either of these oils will make your slime less sticky.
* **Lotion**: a drop of baby lotion or unfragranced body lotion will make your slime stretch further.
* **Baby powder**: for a matte (not glossy) finish.
* **Fragrance oil**: use skin-safe oils that are suitable for making candles, soap and more. Fragranced handwashes can also be used to make slime.

Kitchen bits and pieces

* **Kitchen roll or paper towels**: to wipe up mess and spills.
* **Paper plates and plastic chopping boards**: useful for kneading slime on.
* **Mixing bowls**: a larger bowl is handy for making fluffy slimes or large batches of slime.
* **Mixing utensils**: wooden or metal spoons, spatulas, chopsticks or craft sticks are all great for mixing.

Using and Storing Slime

Slime doesn't come out right every time. Sometimes it depends on the ingredients you use and even how hot or cold your hands or the room is. Try these tips if you're having trouble getting your slime to feel just right.

is your slime...

too hard or dry?

Run the slime under a warm tap, then stretch out the slime so that it absorbs the water. Make sure slime does not go down the plughole.

too sticky?

Add more activator, a few drops at a time, and work in to the slime until it no longer sticks to your fingers.

breaking apart?

A good slime should be soft and stretchy. Add a little hot water, baby oil or body lotion.

itchy?

Some ingredients used in slime can irritate your skin. If any itching or redness occurs, wash your hands and put on protective gloves. Decide whether or not to throw out the slime.

not gelling properly?

Keep mixing for a few minutes until the bonds begin to form. If this doesn't work, then add a little more activator and mix again.

too bad!

Sometimes slime can't be saved! If any of the following has happened to your slime, it is time to throw it out:

- It is starting to smell bad.
- None of the tips above have helped.
- It has changed colour.
- It is more than a few weeks old.

Top Tip!

Place used slime in an old container or bag and put in the bin. Never put slime down sinks or drains.

Storing slime

When you're ready to store your slime, keeping it in an airtight container will stop it drying out and make it last longer. Reuse plastic containers or packaging if you can.

White Slime

Get to grips with making slime by trying this simple recipe – it only contains three ingredients, which you may already have at home.

What You'll Need:

- 250 ml white PVA glue
- liquid laundry detergent
- food colouring or acrylic paint

1

Pour the glue into a bowl. Add drops of food colouring or a good squirt of acrylic paint to brighten up your white slime.

16

2 Add small dashes of laundry detergent, mixing as you go, until the mixture begins to come away from the sides of the bowl.

3 Knead the slime with your hands on a clean work surface until the slime becomes stretchy and no longer sticky.

Remember!
The laundry detergent you use should contain borax (sodium borate). Liquid laundry starch creates a good goo, too!

A handy recipe!

Clear Slime

This clear slime uses contact lens solution and bicarbonate of soda to activate the mixture. It's quick and easy and makes a stretch-tastic slime.

What You'll Need:

* 250 ml clear PVA glue
* contact lens solution
* 1/4 tsp bicarbonate of soda
* food colouring or acrylic paint
* water (optional)
* baby oil or coconut oil (optional)

1

Pour the glue into a bowl and mix.

2

Add the bicarbonate of soda and mix until it has dissolved.

3

Use food colouring or paint for colour, then add the contact lens solution, one generous squirt at a time. Mix well adding a little water if you need to.

4

When the slime is the right consistency, remove it from the bowl, knead and stretch. Use a few drops of baby oil or coconut oil to make the slime less sticky.

Why not try?
Adding some water to add stretch to your clear slime.

Clearly amazing!

Fluffy Slime

For the fluffiest of all the slimes, shaving foam is the secret ingredient that turns ordinary slime into a super-soft cloudlike mixture.

What You'll Need:

* 500 ml white or clear PVA glue
* 125 ml shaving foam
* liquid laundry detergent
* food colouring or acrylic paint

1

Pour the glue into a large mixing bowl. Add the shaving foam and gently fold into the glue.

2 Choose the colour you'd like your slime to be then add some food colouring or paint. Fold in gently until the mixture has completely combined.

3 Add laundry detergent, a dash at a time, and mix well. The mixture should begin to come away from the sides of the bowl.

So soft!

4 Knead the slime on a clean work surface until it reaches a slime consistency. Be gentle to make sure the slime stays fluffy.

Glitter Slime

A gorgeous glittery goo, glitter slime takes just two minutes to make!

What You'll Need:

* 125 ml clear PVA glue or glitter glue
* 30 ml water
* 1/2 tsp bicarbonate of soda
* contact lens solution
* glitter – iridescent ones are so sparkly!

1 Pour the glue and water into a bowl and mix. You can skip step 3 if you use glitter glue!

2 Add the bicarbonate of soda and mix until it has dissolved.

3

Choose your favourite shade of glitter, or mix two colours together into the slime.

4

Next, add squirts of contact lens solution, mixing as you go.

5

Stretch and knead your glitter slime until it is the perfect consistency.

Why not try?
Adding acrylic paint or food colouring for an extra splash of colour.

So sparkly!

Confetti Slime

Celebrate any occasion with this pretty slime. It's brilliant to give as a birthday present, though remember it's not an edible gift!

What you'll Need:

* 250 ml white PVA glue
* 60 ml shaving foam
* liquid laundry detergent
* pink food colouring
* hundreds and thousands

1

Pour the glue into a bowl. Add the shaving foam, folding it gently into the glue.

2

Add dashes of laundry detergent, mixing as you go, until you have a fluffy slime consistency.

3

Fold in drops of food colouring until your slime is perfectly pink, then knead it with your hands.

4

Sprinkle hundreds and thousands of hundreds and thousands into the slime!

Time to celebrate!

Crunchy Slime

Treat your eyes and ears to a slime sensation like no other with this crunchy slime. It's perfect for squishing your worries away!

What You'll Need:

* 250 ml clear PVA glue
* 30 ml water
* contact lens solution
* ¼ tsp bicarbonate of soda
* food colouring
* clear glass beads

It's crunch time!

1

Pour the glue and the water into a bowl and mix well.

Stir in some drops of food colouring, adding more until you have your chosen colour, then mix in the bicarbonate of soda.

3

Add your beads to the bowl – enough to cover the surface of the slime – then mix well.

4

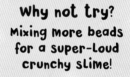

Why not try?
Mixing more beads for a super-loud crunchy slime!

Mix in squirts of contact lens solution until your mixture turns into a slime consistency. Then knead the slime on a clean work surface.

Make some noise!

27

Crunchy Foam Slime

Fluffy and crunchy slime? Whip up a large batch, as everyone will want a squish!

What You'll Need:

- 500 ml white PVA glue
- 120 ml shaving foam
- liquid laundry detergent
- small coloured foam balls

1

Pour the glue into a bowl. Add a couple of squirts of shaving foam and fold it gently into the glue.

2

Add a small amount of laundry detergent and mix well. Add more detergent to activate the slime, as needed.

3

Knead the mixture until it turns into a slime consistency.

4

Add the foam balls and fold the mixture with your hands until everything has combined. Simple!

Cute and colourful!

Highlighter Slime

You'll never find a cooler use for your highlighters! This glowing slime is bound to impress.

What You'll Need:

- 125 ml clear PVA glue
- 30 ml water
- 1/2 tsp bicarbonate of soda
- contact lens solution
- non-toxic highlighter pen or pens

1

Pour the glue and water into a bowl and mix.

2

Add the bicarbonate of soda and stir until it has dissolved.

3

Next, add the contact lens solution, one tablespoon at a time. Mix well and knead until your slime is spot on!

4

Make sure your work surface is covered, choose a highlighter pen, then get colouring!

5

Fold and knead the slime until the colour has spread evenly. Then stretch and squeeze!

The highlight of your slime collection!

Why not try?
Using different coloured highlighter pens for a magical neon look.

Metallic Slime

The addition of metallic paint turns this slime gorgeously gold — to a goo of pure luxury! You can swap the activators for liquid laundry starch if you'd like.

What You'll Need:

* 250 ml clear PVA glue
* 30 ml water
* contact lens solution
* ¼ tsp bicarbonate of soda
* metallic acrylic paint
* water (optional)
* baby oil or coconut oil (optional)

1 Pour the clear glue and water into a bowl and mix well.

2 Add the bicarbonate of soda and mix until it has dissolved.

3 Squirt in a generous amount of metallic paint, then mix until the mixture begins to come away from the sides of the bowl.

4 Knead the mixture until you have a gold-standard slime consistency!

Why not try? Adding glitter for a truly glistening slime, or twisting two metallic slimes together.

As good as gold!

Pompom Slime

A fun slime that you won't want to put down! So easy, so stretchy!

What You'll Need:

- 125 ml clear PVA glue
- 30 ml water
- $\frac{1}{2}$ tsp bicarbonate of soda
- contact lens solution
- pompoms (different colours and sizes work well)

1

Pour the glue and water into a bowl and mix.

2

Add the bicarbonate of soda and stir until it has dissolved.

3

Next, add the contact lens solution, one squirt at a time. Mix well and knead until the slime is the right consistency.

4

Toss in your pompoms, folding them into the mixture with your hands.

Pom, pom, pom!

Sparkly Star Slime

Adding tiny star sequins to ordinary clear slime will turn your mixture into a superstar of a slime! Try this twinkly recipe for yourself!

What You'll Need:

* ✶ 125 ml clear PVA glue
* ✶ 30 ml water
* ✶ ¼ tsp bicarbonate of soda
* ✶ contact lens solution
* ✶ star sequins

1

Pour the glue into a bowl. Add the water and mix well.

2

Add the bicarbonate of soda and stir until it has dissolved.

3

Next, add the contact lens solution, one tablespoon at a time. Mix well and knead until the slime is the right consistency.

Why not try?

A slime upgrade – adding just a couple more ingredients will transform this goo into gorgeous Galaxy Slime (see pages 50-51)!

4

Pour some star sequins into the bowl – two different colours of sequins look lovely! Mix and stretch your starry slime.

Twinkle, twinkle slimy stars!

Alphabet Slime

Supposed to be doing your homework? Here's a cool new way to practise your spellings!

What You'll Need:

- 150 ml clear PVA glue
- 60 ml water
- contact lens solution
- 1 packet alphabet beads

1

Pour the glue into a mixing bowl.

2 Add the water and mix well with a spatula or spoon.

3 Squirt in some contact lens solution. Stir until the mixture turns into a slime texture, adding more solution if you need to.

Glitter will take this slime to the next level!

4 Tip in a packet of alphabet beads – the more letters, the better! Look out for words that may magically appear in the slime, or try to spell out your name!

Why not try?
Using your favourite beads for a slime that's as unique as you are!

Scented Slime

Adding a scent to the mix will take your slime to the next level. Lemon, strawberry or even chocolate are all great scents, or choose your favourite fragrance!

What You'll Need:

* 100 ml white PVA glue
* ¼ tsp bicarbonate of soda
* contact lens solution
* scented liquid handwash

1

Pour the white glue into a bowl.

2

Mix together the bicarbonate of soda, with squirts of contact lens solution until you have a slime consistency.

3

Add some handwash (we used chocolate orange), one squirt at a time, and mix well. The slime should become smooth and glossy.

4

When the slime is ready, remove it from the bowl. Sniff it, stretch it and let it slide through your fingers!

Smells divine!

Why not try?
Substituting a skin-safe fragrance oil or candle scent for the handwash, then adding food colouring to colour your slime.

Gingerbread Slime

Another favourite scented slime is this gorgeous gingerbread goo. While it smells amazing, remember that it's just for PLAY!

What You'll Need:

* 100 ml white PVA glue
* ¼ tsp bicarbonate of soda
* contact lens solution
* 1 tsp each of cinnamon and ginger
* biscuit cutters
* glitter (optional)

1

Pour the white glue into a bowl.

42

2 Add the bicarbonate of soda, then squirts of contact lens solution, mixing until the goo comes away from the sides of the bowl.

3 Mix in a teaspoon of cinnamon and a teaspoon of ginger.

4 Your finished slime should smell deliciously spicy! Add some glitter if you like.

Choose your cutest cutters!

Why not try?
Switching the contact lens solution and bicarbonate of soda activators for liquid laundry starch.

Unicorn Snot Slime

This stretch-tastic slime is lovingly known as unicorn snot! It's not as yucky as it sounds.

What You'll Need:

- 125 ml clear PVA glue
- 30 ml water
- 1/2 tsp bicarbonate of soda
- bright green paint
- contact lens solution

1

Add the glue to a bowl.

2

Pour in the water and mix well.

3

Stir in the bicarbonate of soda, which will thicken the slime.

4

Pour in enough paint to make the mixture turn bright green.

5

Mix in squirts of contact lens solution until the slime pulls away easily from sides of the bowl.

Why not try?

Using a tape measure, see how far you can stretch this slime.

Atchoo!

45

Unicorn Poop Slime

A wondrous slime in pretty pastel colours, is unicorn (or unicorn poop!) slime the most gorgeous goo you'll ever create?

What you'll Need:

- large batch of fluffy slime
- purple, pink and pearl-white iridescent paints
- 3 bowls or containers
- glitter or sequins (optional)

1

Divide a large batch of fluffy white slime into three equal parts. Using a clean bowl for each colour, squirt in paint and mix until you have the shade you want. Knead the coloured slimes, one at a time.

Wash your hands after kneading each batch to stop the colours from transferring.

2

Roll the colours into sausage-like pieces and gently press them together.

3

Stretch and twist your slime, taking care not to mix the colours completely.

4

Shake on some extra glitter or sequins to give your slime a magical shimmer!

A legendary slime!

Mermaid Slime

Ever wished you could live under the sea? This ocean-themed slime could be your favourite new goo!

What You'll Need:

* 125 ml clear PVA glue
* 30 ml water
* 1/4 tsp bicarbonate of soda
* holographic blue acrylic paint
* contact lens solution
* shells and pearls
* glitter (optional)

1

Add the clear PVA glue to a bowl, pour in the water, then mix well.

2

Mix in the bicarbonate of soda until it has dissolved.

3

Pour in some paint and mix well. Add more paint until you have the shade that you want. Glitter can be added now too.

4

Mix in squirts of contact lens solution until the mixture comes away from the sides of the bowl. Knead the slime until you have the perfect consistency.

5

Choose any ocean-themed items to add to your slime – shells and pearls work well.

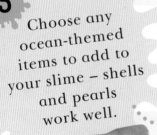

Stretch your slime and channel your inner mermaid!

Galaxy Slime

We're sure there's space in your collection for this stellar slime – it's the greatest slime in the universe!

What You'll Need:

* ✶ 500 ml clear PVA glue or glitter glue
* ✶ 60 ml water
* ✶ ¼ tsp bicarbonate of soda
* ✶ contact lens solution
* ✶ star sequins
* ✶ black acrylic paint
* ✶ purple iridescent acrylic paint

1 Pour the glue into a bowl. Add the water and mix well.

2 Add the bicarbonate of soda and mix until it has dissolved.

3 Next, add squirts of contact lens solution. Mix well and knead until the slime is the right consistency.

Out of this world!

4 Pour some star sequins into the bowl, then add a large squirt of purple paint and a tiny squirt of black paint. Fold the mixture gently, taking care not to mix up the colours completely.

Why not try?
Adding a little more water to make your slime super stretchy.

Colour-Changing Slime

This colour-changing slime is as cool as a chameleon! Heat it up and cool it down to see this slime's true colours!

What You'll Need:

* 125 ml clear PVA glue
* ¼ tsp bicarbonate of soda
* 1 tbsp liquid laundry detergent
* acrylic paint
* ¼ tsp colour-changing nail pigment powder

1 Pour the glue into a mixing bowl.

2 Add the bicarbonate of soda. Mix until it dissolves.

3 Next, add a squirt of laundry detergent and mix in some acrylic paint.

4 Once the mixture starts to come together, add the nail pigment powder. Knead the slime with your hands until it's no longer sticky.

Ask an adult to find nail pigment powder online - it works better than heat-sensitive paint.

5 Warm your hands, then press down on the slime for incredible results!

Hands down the coolest slime!

Why not try?
Dipping the slime into a bowl of iced water, or heating it with a hairdryer to reveal the different shades.

Magnetic Slime

You're bound to be attracted to this slime recipe! Find the supplies online to make one of the coolest slimes around.

What You'll Need:

- 500 ml white PVA glue
- 100 ml shaving foam
- 150 g iron filings
- liquid laundry detergent
- silver glitter
- strong (neodymium) magnet

1

Pour the glue into a large mixing bowl, then gently fold in the shaving foam.

2 Next, ask an adult to add the iron filings (it's a messy job). Stir well.

The more iron filings you add, the stronger the magnetic pull!

3 Mix in the sparkly glitter.

4 Add small amounts of laundry detergent and keep stirring until the mixture comes away from the sides of the bowl.

5 Knead and stretch the slime with your hands until you have the perfect slime consistency.

6 Place the slime on a covered surface or an old plate, then use a strong magnet (or magnets) to test how the slime reacts.

Magical Rainbow Slime

This colourful slime will really wow your friends and family – it's one of the prettiest slimes around! Take care not to overmix the colours, or the slime may go brown.

What You'll Need:

- 1 large batch of fluffy slime
- food colouring or paint for each rainbow colour
- 7 slime containers
- glitter (optional)

1

Start by making a large batch of white fluffy slime (the recipe is on pages 20–21).

56

2 Divide up the slime into seven small containers – one for each rainbow colour. Add drops of food colouring or paint to each pot. Knead the colours one at a time, adding more colouring, until you have the shades you want.

Wash your hands after kneading each batch to stop the colours from running.

3 Roll the colours into long pieces, then press them together, as shown.

4 Now stretch out the colours to create a cool rainbow shape or carefully squish them together.

Why not try? Adding some glitter to make your slime even more magical!

Go colour crazy!

Butter Slime

This buttery slime is super-smooth and spreadable, thanks to its special ingredient – modelling clay. Try it for yourself – just not on your toast!

What You'll Need:

* 250 ml white PVA glue
* 250 ml air-drying modelling clay
* 250 ml shaving foam
* 1 tsp bicarbonate of soda
* yellow food colouring or acrylic paint

Moo!

1

Pour the white PVA glue into the mixing bowl. Add the shaving foam and mix well.

2

Add the bicarbonate of soda. Mix until it dissolves.

3

Add the contact lens solution, a teaspoon at a time, mixing as you go. Once the slime begins to form, knead the mixture with your hands until it's no longer sticky.

4

Take a piece of modelling clay and mould into a disc shape. Place it on your slime and fold and mix the slime in on itself until the clay has combined. The texture should become buttery smooth!

Spread this instead!

Why not try?
Adding some body lotion if your slime is too crumbly – ideally one that's not too glossy.

59

Kinetic Slime

Sculpt it, mould it, roll it, move it! Add kinetic play sand to form a slime that will stretch like a goo and squish like a dough!

What You'll Need:

* 75 ml white PVA glue
* 75 ml liquid laundry starch
* kinetic play sand

1

Pour the glue into a bowl.

2

Add some coloured kinetic sand, one tablespoon at a time. Stir well until you have thick, sandy mixture.

3

Mix in the laundry starch, one tablespoon at a time. When your mixture turns to dough and is no longer sticky, remove the slime from the bowl.

4

Squeeze and knead the slime until it's ready for some kinetic slime action!

Slime or dough – do you know?

Why not try?

Using normal play sand and acrylic paint if you don't have any kinetic sand to hand.

Bubblegum Slime

Take your slime experiments to the next level with this fun party trick. How big will your bubble grow before it pops?

What You'll Need:

* 1 batch of slime
* 1 plastic straw
* food colouring or paint

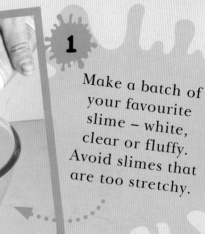

1

Make a batch of your favourite slime – white, clear or fluffy. Avoid slimes that are too stretchy.

2

Add some colour – we like bubblegum pink!

While holding a ball of slime on your hand, place a straw into the slime.

3

While this slime may sound tasty it's definitely not edible. Don't suck slime through the straw or be tempted to chew on this recipe!

4

Support the slime with your hand and blow hard into the straw. A slime bubble should begin to form – keep blowing until you have a bubblegum-sized bubble!

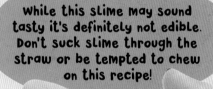

Bubble-licious!

Valentine's Slime

Love is in the slime! Show someone how you really feel with this romantic recipe!

What You'll Need:

- ♥ 125 ml clear PVA glue
- ♥ 30 ml water
- ♥ ¼ tsp bicarbonate of soda
- ♥ red or pink glitter
- ♥ love heart sequins

1

Pour the glue and water into a bowl and mix.

2 Add the bicarbonate of soda and mix until it has dissolved.

3 Next, add the contact lens solution, one tablespoon at a time. Mix well and knead until your slime is ready.

4 Mix in some Valentine-themed glitter and sequins using your hands.

Share the love!

Spring Slime

How cute is this seasonal slime? Make it at the start of spring to celebrate a brand-new season! Use clear glue to show off the sparkle.

What You'll Need:

* 150 ml clear PVA glue
* 60 ml water
* glitter
* yellow food colouring
* contact lens solution
* decorative chicks

1

Pour the glue into a mixing bowl. Add the water and stir well.

2

Add a few squirts of food colouring (we used gel colouring) until your mixture is nice and bright.

3

Throw some chicks into the mix!

4

Add a teaspoon of contact lens solution, then mix and knead until you have the perfect slime consistency!

Hello, yellow!

Why not try?
Adding flower sequins in place of the chicks to create an equally cheerful spring slime.

Spooky Slime

This spooky slime really does glow in the dark! It's perfect for trick or treating!

What You'll Need:

* 125 ml clear PVA glue
* 60 ml water
* ½ tsp bicarbonate of soda
* glow-in-the-dark paint or ¼ tsp glow-in-the-dark powder
* contact lens solution
* mini plastic spiders or Halloween sequins

1

Add the glue to a bowl, then pour in the water and mix well.

8

2

Stir in the bicarbonate of soda, which will thicken the slime.

3

Stir in the glow-in-the-dark paint or powder.

4

Add squirts of contact lens solution and stir until the slime pulls away easily from sides of the bowl.

Mix in some plastic spiders for added creepiness.

5

Eeek!

Ready, steady, glow!

Slimy fact!

The glow occurs when electrons in the slime absorb energy from light. Find a sunny place to charge up your slime, before playing with it in a dark place.

Festive Slime

Deck the halls with slimes of holly! This glittery clear slime is guaranteed to get you in the festive mood!

What You'll Need:

* 125 ml clear PVA glue
* 125 ml water
* 1/2 tsp bicarbonate of soda
* green glitter or glitter glue
* contact lens solution
* festive sequins

1

Add the glue to a bowl, then pour in the water and mix well.

2

Stir in the bicarbonate of soda to thicken the slime.

Use some green glitter to make your slime sparkle and mix well.

4

Next add 1 tablespoon of contact lens solution. Stir the slime well until it pulls away easily from the sides of the bowl. Add more solution if you need to.

A very merry slime!

5

Choose some jolly sequins to mix in, then stretch and squish!

Why not try?
Choosing your favourite festive sequins - snowflakes, snowmen or Christmas trees!

Slime Pulling

Looking for a new way to play? Try your hand at slime pulling for an awesome slime sensation!

What You'll Need:

* batch of slime
* old tennis or badminton racquet or a gridded utensil such as a potato masher
* food colouring or paint

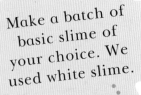

1

Make a batch of basic slime of your choice. We used white slime.

2

Add food colouring or paint and mix. When your slime is ready, place it on a paper plate or covered worktop.

3

Grab a racquet or a potato masher and press down firmly over the slime.

4

Pull up slowly to stretch your slime. It's a super-satisfying slime experience!

Super relaxing!

Why not try?
Experimenting with different shades of slimes for a cool colour combo.

73

Slime Bracelets

Beautiful bracelets you'll want to wear and share! Choose slime colours that match your favourite outfits.

What You'll Need:

- batch of clear slime
- 3 containers
- food colouring or paints
- glitter
- jumbo craft sticks
- deep lids from jars

1

Make a batch of clear slime (the recipe is on pages 18–19), then divide the slime into three equal parts.

2

Using a clean bowl for each colour, add paint and glitter and mix until you have your desired shade. Knead the coloured slimes, one at a time, then store in sealed containers.

3

Ask an adult to boil some craft sticks in a pan for 30 minutes, until the sticks are soft and bendy. Boil more sticks than you need, as they break easily!

4

Pat the sticks dry, and, very carefully, bend each stick and mould it into a deep lid. Leave to dry for 24–48 hours.

5

Remove the craft stick from the lid, then mould a thin piece of slime large enough to cover both sides of the stick.

Awesome accessories!

75

Aqua Slime

This fishy slime recipe uses shampoo and salt as its base – great if you've run out of glue or activators!

What You'll Need:

- 250 ml clear or blue shampoo
- 1/8 tsp salt
- blue food colouring (optional)
- small jam jar
- plastic fish toys or fish-shaped beads

1

Pour the shampoo into a bowl. If your shampoo is clear, stir in some drops of blue food colouring, until you have a rich blue colour.

2

Add 1/8 teaspoon (or a very small pinch) of salt and mix well.

3

Pour the mixture into a clean jam jar, then add a fish bead or two on top.

Fabulously fishy!

4

Screw on the lid tightly, then transfer your slime to the fridge overnight. The next day, the slime will have firmed up.

Why not try?
Making a giant slime aquarium, adding more fishy friends.

Slime Pets

Slime pets are a fun way to store your slime. Choose containers of different shapes and sizes, and give each slimy friend a name!

What You'll Need:

- batches of freshly made slime
- airtight glass or plastic containers
- white or clear PVA glue
- craft materials, such as googly eyes, pipe cleaners and fairy cake cases
- marker pens

1

Choose clean jam jars or baby-food jars and press your slime inside. Screw on each lid tightly.

2

Stick on a single, a pair or even more googly eyes!

3

Draw on more details with permanent marker pens.

4

Add extra details using whatever craft materials you have at home. Pipe-cleaner arms, perhaps?

Forever friends!

Slimy tip!
Slime can keep for several weeks in an airtight container. Warm up slime in your hands if you've not played with it for a while and add a little water or more activator if you need to.

79

Slime Stress Ball

Squeeze your troubles away with this squishy stress ball that's filled with slime! It's a great way to unwind.

What You'll Need:

- batch of stretchy slime (clear or white)
- 1 balloon
- small funnel
- chopstick
- marker pens

1

Find a fistful of slime that you've previously made. Do not use any slime that has an odour or has any sign of mould. The slime should still be stretchy – add some water if you need to.

2

Stretch out the balloon, taking care not to make any holes, then place the funnel in the neck of the balloon.

3 Place small blobs of slime in the funnel, then carefully push them into the balloon using your fingers and a chopstick. This will take a little patience!

4 When the balloon is filled to about the size of your palm, tie a knot in the end.

5 Draw a design on your stress ball using marker pens. We chose a happy emoticon!

Now squeeze and relax!

Why not try?
Pressing your stress ball through a small net to make tiny slime bubbles appear!

Slime Suncatcher

This slime decoration will make any window instantly more beautiful. Hang it proudly and let your slime catch some rays!

What You'll Need:

* glitter slime
* shallow plastic lid (from a food container)

1

Take some glitter slime from a batch you have previously made. It should be about the size of a ping-pong ball, and ideally have two or more different colours of glitter.

2 Press the slime into the lid, making sure not to leave any gaps.

3 Leave the lid in a warm place for at least 24 hours. As it dries, the slime should form a disc shape. Peel the disc from the lid.

4 Stick your suncatcher on a window. As sunlight shines through, colours will brighten up your room!

Make your window look wonderful!

Gummy Bear Slime

A slime made from gummies that's delicious and yummy! This edible slime is easy to make and safe to eat – whip up a batch to share with friends.

What You'll Need:

* 150 g gummy bears
* 50 g icing sugar
* 50 g cornflour
* 1 tsp coconut oil (optional)

!

?

1

Choose colours of gummy bears that go well together, then place them in a microwave-safe bowl.

2 Ask an adult to heat the gummy bears in a microwave for 15 seconds at a time. Stir well and reheat as needed until you have a smooth gummy mixture.

The bowl will be hot so handle with care!

3 Stir in the cornflour and icing sugar a tablespoon at a time, until the mixture begins to form a dough.

4 As the dough cools down, knead it with your hands. Too sticky? Rub a little coconut oil on your hands.

5 When the mixture reaches a stretchy consistency, your gummy slime is ready – sniff it, stretch it, squish it and taste it!

A slimy sweet treat!

Why not try? Making gummy slime in different colours? Edible glitter adds extra sparkle!

Chocolate Slime

Another slime that's totally edible and completely delicious! Perfect for anyone with a sweet tooth – be sure to brush yours afterwards!

What You'll Need:

- 397 g condensed milk
- 50 g chocolate
- icing sugar
- cornflour
- 1 tbsp cocoa

1

Pour the condensed milk into a heat-proof bowl, then break the chocolate into pieces and add to the bowl.

2 Ask an adult to place the bowl over a pan of boiling water and simmer on a low heat.

3 Stir the mixture until the chocolate has melted, then take the pan off the heat.

The bowl will be hot so handle with care!

4 When the mixture has cooled a little, add a tablespoon of cocoa to produce a dark, chocolate colour. Then stir in tablespoons of icing sugar and cornflour in turn until you have a smooth, sticky slime that smells amazing!

Chocs away!

Spaghetti Slime

Here's another slime that you can stretch, sniff and even taste! Get yourself in a tangle with this messy spaghetti slime.

What You'll Need:

- 250 g dried spaghetti
- 3 colours of food colouring
- sunflower or vegetable oil
- water

1

Divide the spaghetti into three parts – one for each colour.

2

Ask an adult to place one section of the spaghetti in a pan of boiling water, then pour in a teaspoon of your first food colouring. Boil the spaghetti according to the instructions on the packet.

3

Ask an adult to drain the cooked spaghetti in a colander. Wash it with cold water, then drain again.

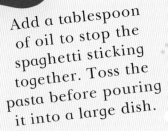

The spaghetti will be hot - handle with care!

4 Add a tablespoon of oil to stop the spaghetti sticking together. Toss the pasta before pouring it into a large dish.

5 Repeat steps 1–4 for each colour, until you have three colours of spaghetti in the dish.

Oodles of noodles!

Why not try... making a colourful friendship bracelet from your spaghetti!

Glossary

* **acrylic paint**
  A fast-drying paint containing an artificial acrylic substance.

* **activator**
  A liquid or powder that turns the liquid glue mixture into the consistency of slime.

* **borax**
  A natural mineral that is used for cleaning, often found in laundry products. Borax also is known as sodium borate, sodium tetraborate or disodium tetraborate.

* **iridescent**
  Luminous colours that change when you look at them from different angles.

* **kinetic play sand**
  Modelling sand that contains silicone. It can be easily moulded and does not dry out.

* **neodymium magnet**
  A very strong magnet made from neodymium, a soft silvery metal.

* **polymer**
  Large molecules that are made when many smaller molecules join together, end-to-end. Most types of slime are examples of polymers.

* **PVA (polyvinyl acetate)**
  A clear or white type of glue with a rubbery texture.

Credits

With thanks to **Abigael Longfellow, PastelSlimesUK**

While every effort has been made to credit all contributors, we would like to apologize should there be any omissions or errors, and would be pleased to make any appropriate corrections for future editions of this book.

Cloud King Creative: 5tl, 6tl, 12b, 13tr, 54b, 57t, 57cl, 57cr, 57b, 63cl, 63cr, 63b, 90tl, 92br, 93bl.

istock.com: 18t, 23b, 30-31, 62, 86t.

Shutterstock.com: 1, 3c, 5, 6, 7, 56, 74-75, 90c, 91t, 91c, 91b, 92c Cinch; 2-3, 94-95 Lariem; 5tr, 7br, 12tr, 92-93t Keizerphoto133; 5cl, 5bl, 7cl, 8b, 72-73t, 90tl, 92tr, 92bl, 96 Bret Skagerberg; 8t, 9t, 11c, 14bl, 19bl jarabee123; 8-9c travel addict; forton 9c, 17b forton; 10-11 lliveinoctober; 13cl, 14br Africa Studio; Apple's Eye Studio 13cr, 15t; 15b Good Shop Background; 16t, 16c, 17tr Sudowoodo; 20t mhatzapa; 22tl, 22tr, 22br, 23tr Shyshell; 24-25t mayakova; 24-25 Ana Angelova; 26tl, 26tr, 26c, 27cr Margarita_V; 36t, 60-61 Marina May; 38tl, 38br Ramon Espelt Photography; 38c Rose Carson; 38tr Mega Pixel; 42t, 42bl, 43cr, 43br sarashowalter; 44t, 45br Daria Voskoboeva; 45bl Pressmaster; 46t Alex708; 48-49 Marish; 50t Saiana; 52 Nadia Snopek; 58-59 los_ojos_pardos; 66-67 MyImages – Micha; 68-69 FARBAI; 70-71 olllikeballoon; 76-77 gst, 78-79 Pinar Ince; 80-81 Reamolko; 81b katarinag; 84-85 Davor Djopar.

Index